THIS IS YOUR JOURNEY

Comforting Words After Pregnancy Loss

by Lori E Collins

LEEDSWOOD PRESS

PUBLISHED BY LEEDSWOOD PRESS

ISBN-10: 0-9989165-0-1
ISBN-13: 978-0-9989165-0-7

If you light a lamp for someone else, it will also brighten your path.
—Buddha

This is your journey.

No one has lived your experience.

Even though miscarriages are relatively common,
this is something that has happened to you.

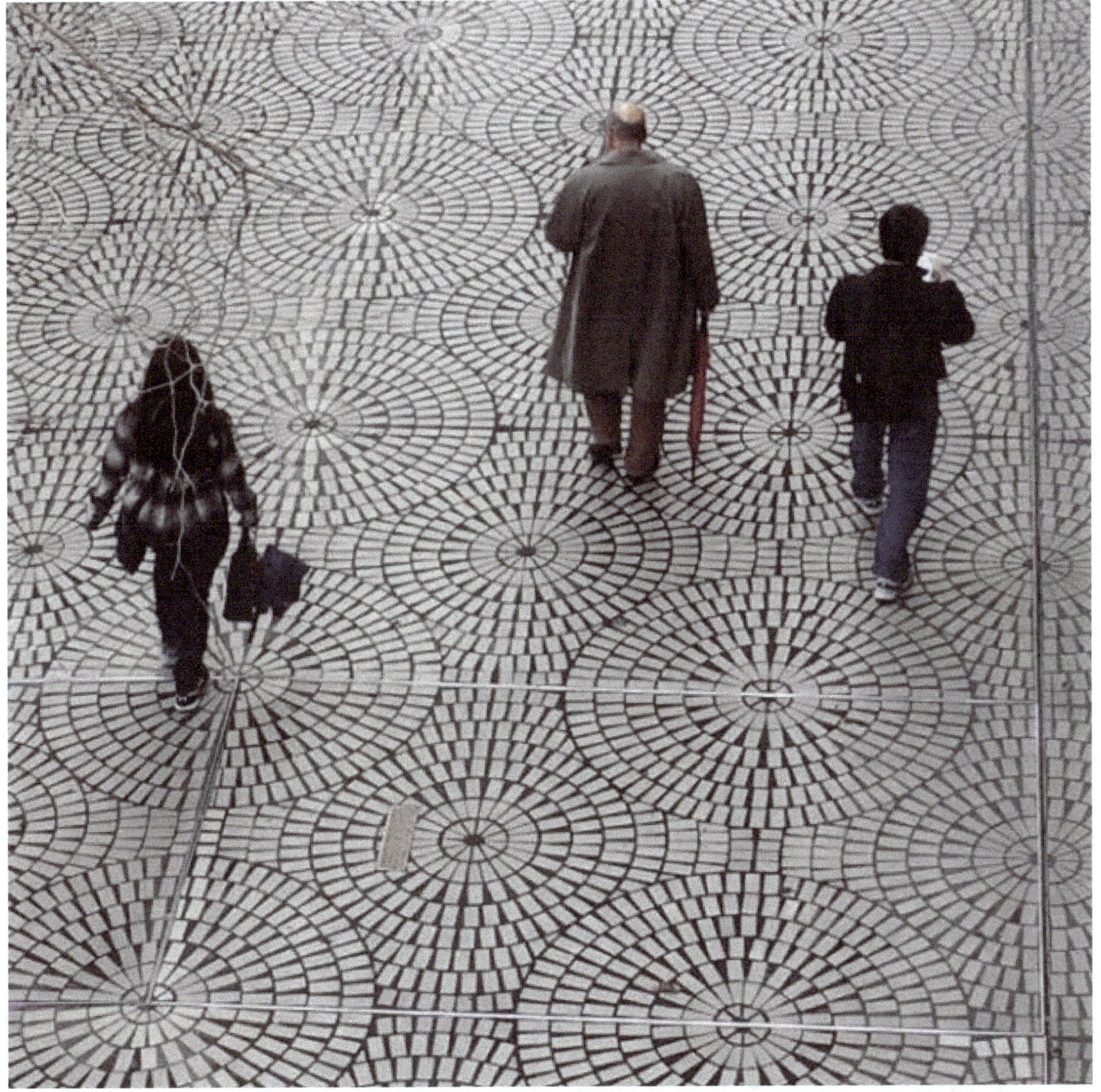

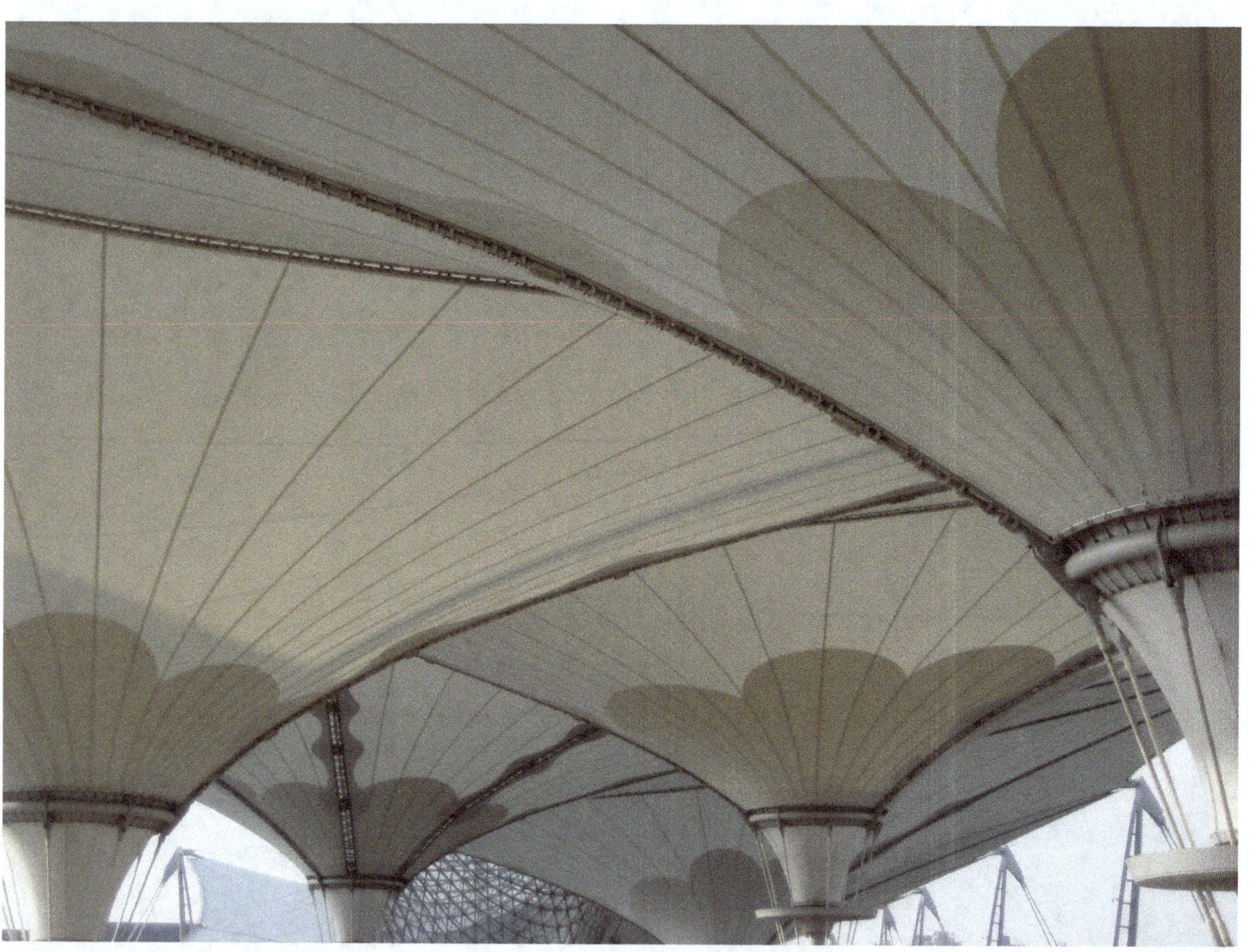

You could encounter a range of emotions.

You might be confused.
You might be grateful.
You might be angry.

Let yourself feel whatever it is you're feeling.
There is no right or wrong.

This is your journey.

If it helps, share your thoughts with someone.

Express yourself through writing or the creation of artwork.

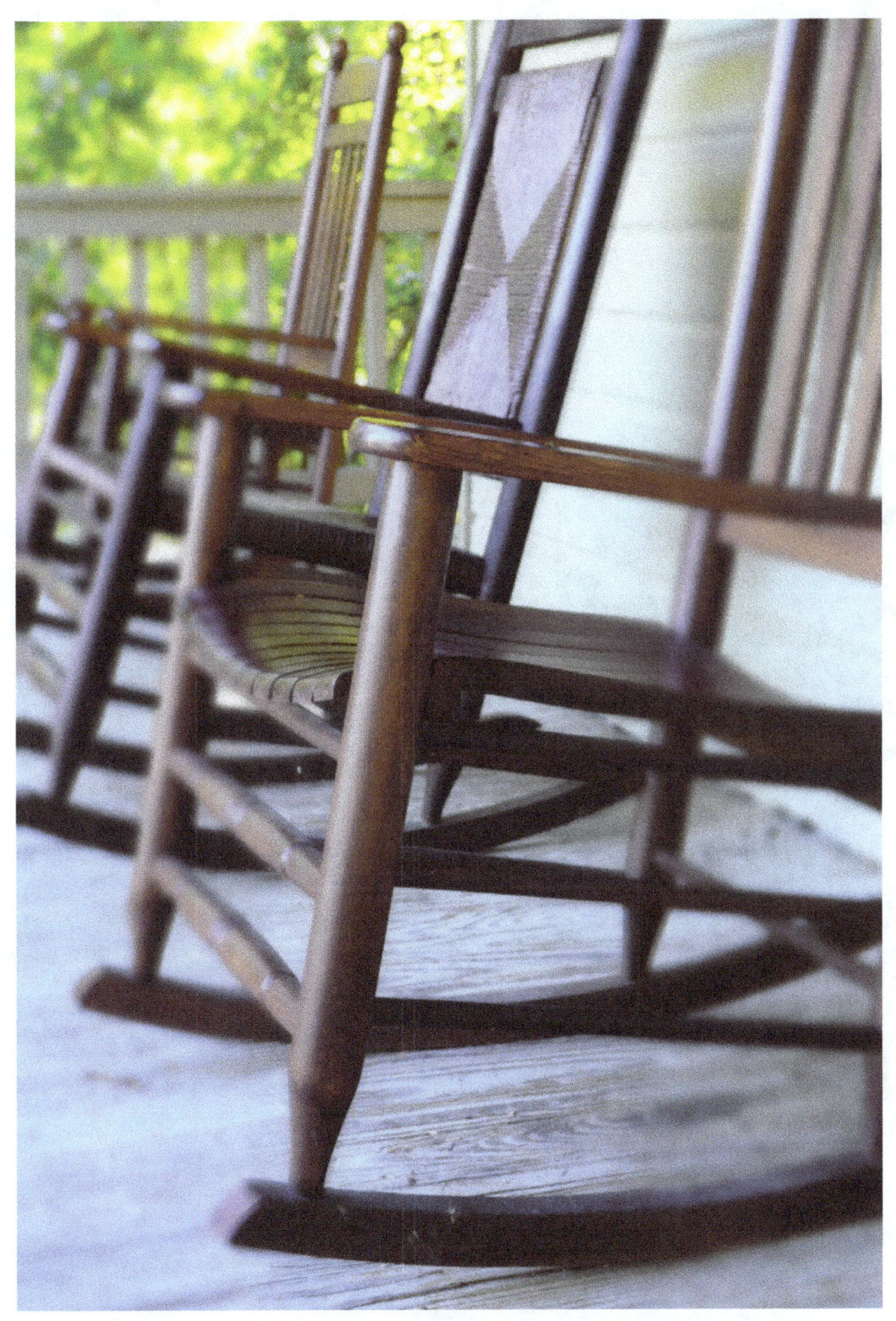

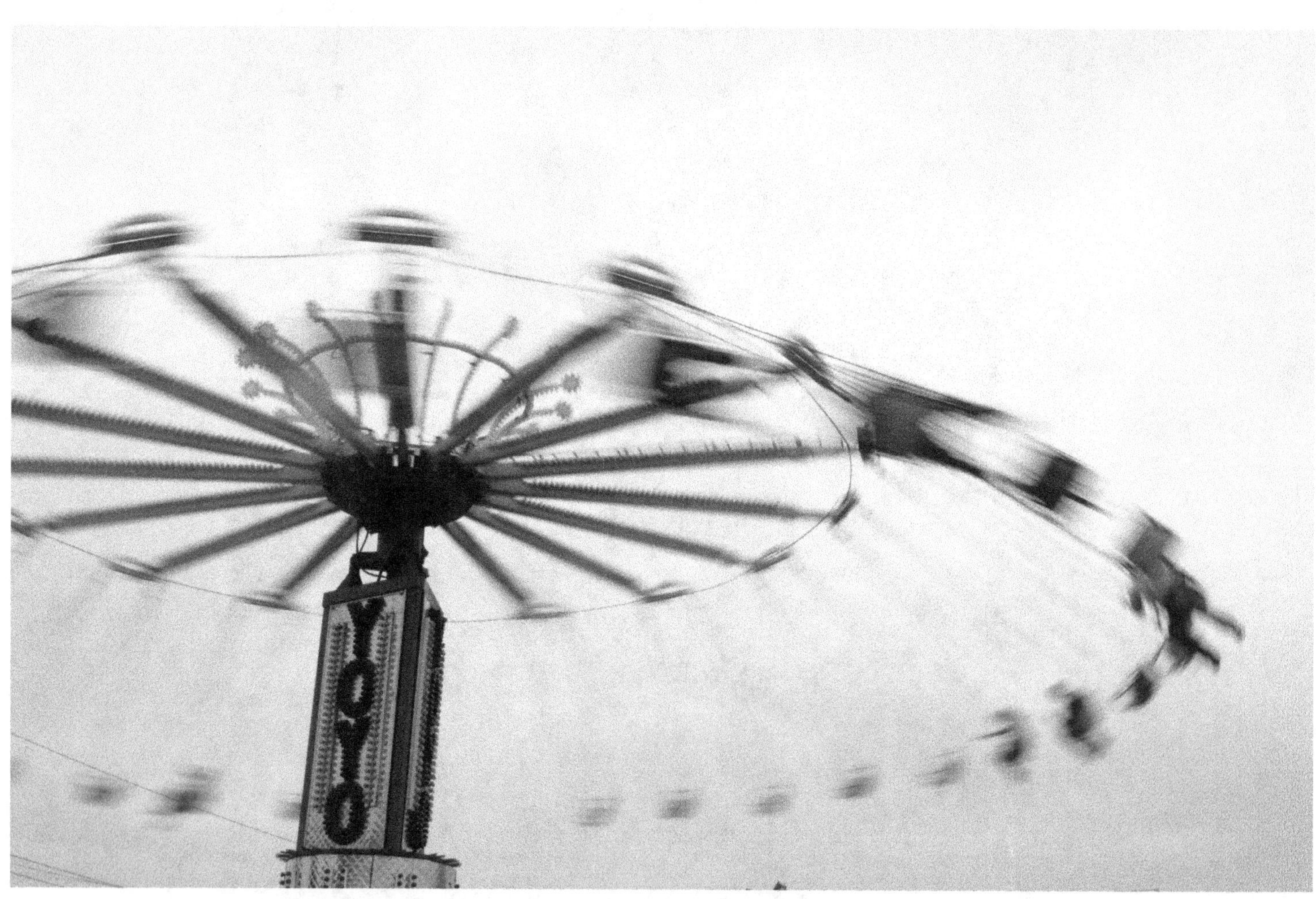

The ground beneath you may feel shaky.

Hang on.

Whether you were newly pregnant or eighteen weeks along,
your feeling of loss is valid.

Your grief is your own.

This is your journey.

Be fully in the present.

Know that you are secure.

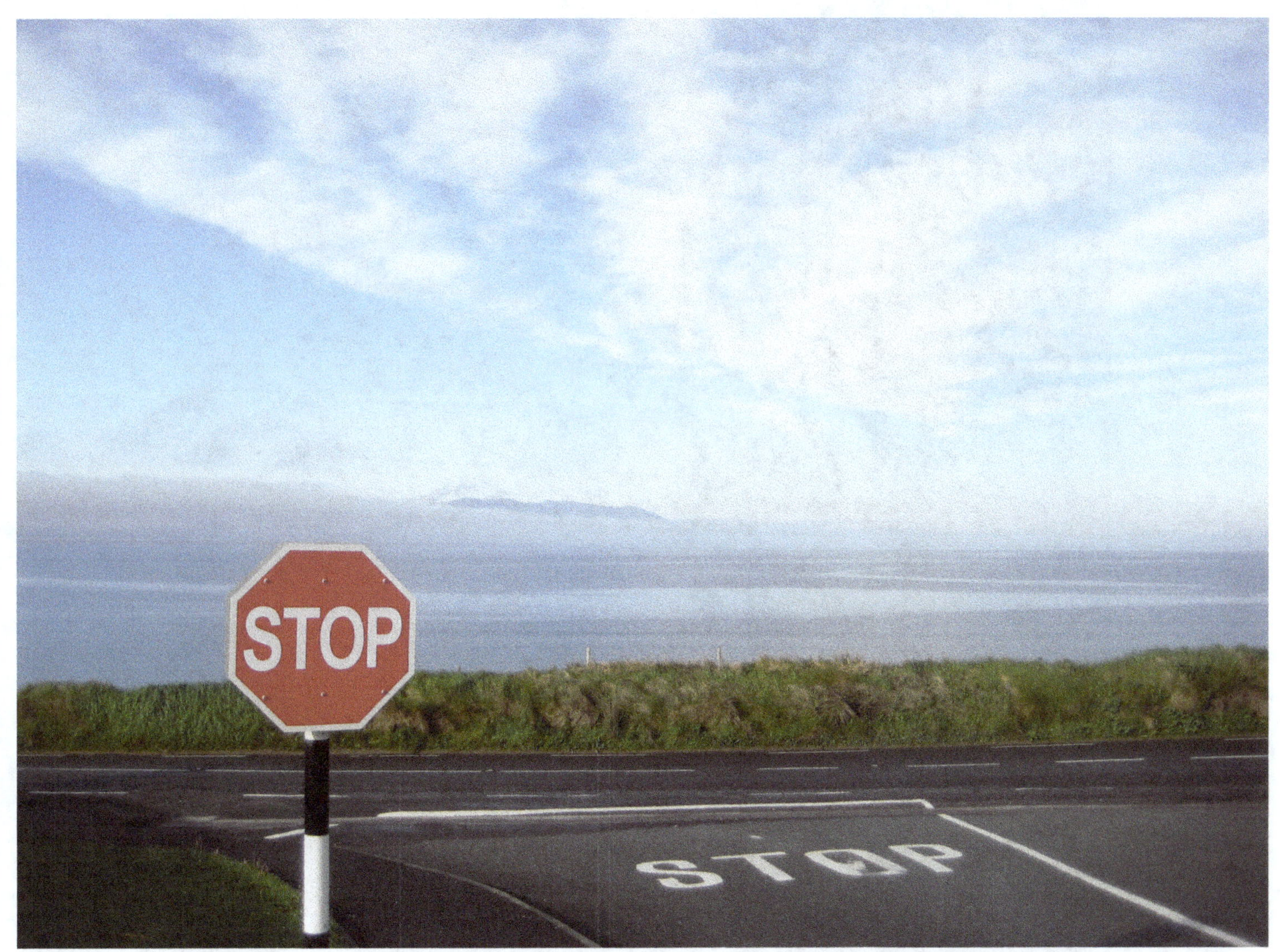
STOP
STOP

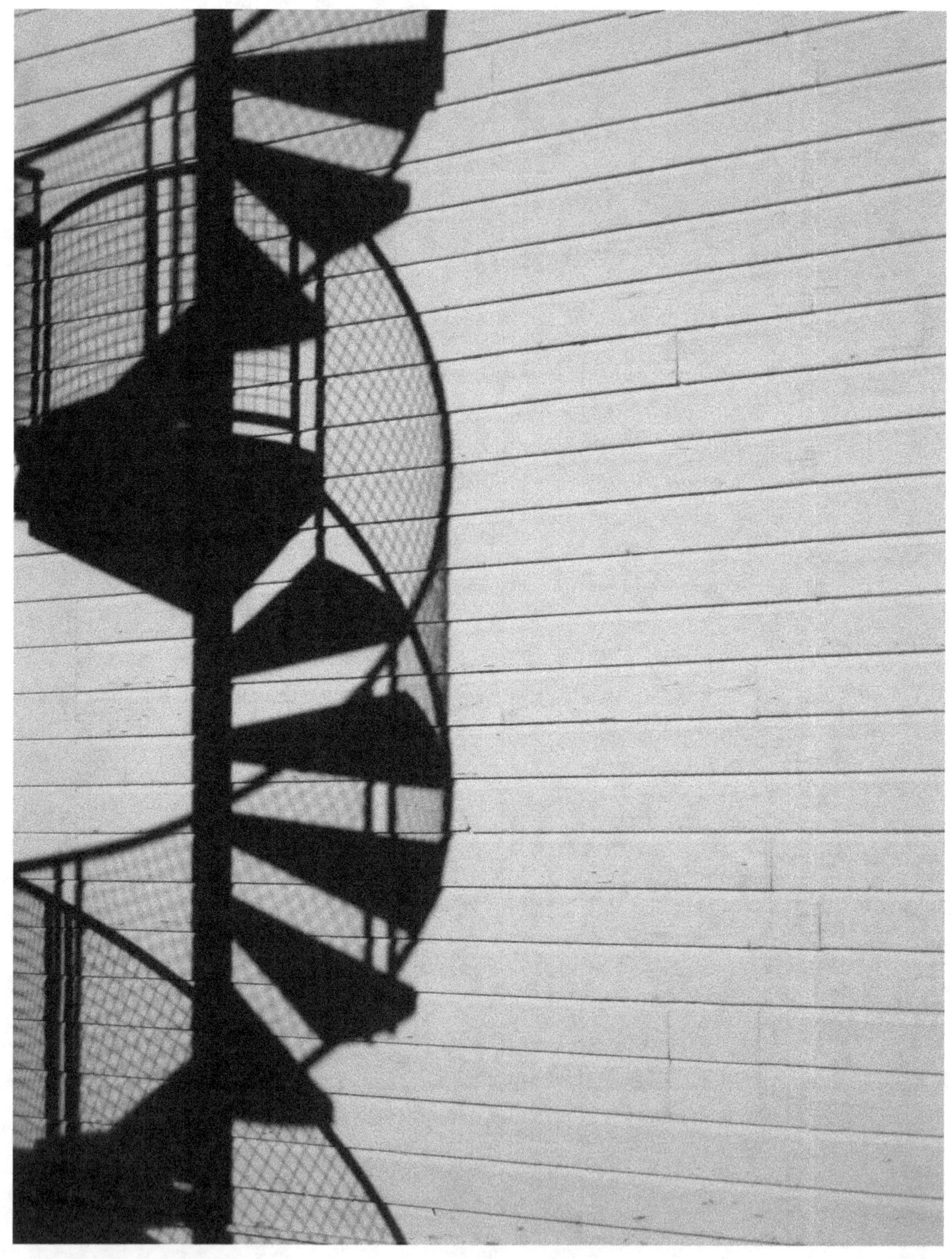

Do not let anyone minimize your pain.

This is not how it was supposed to go.

Only you and your partner can navigate the path from here.

Don't feel rushed to take the next step.

This is your journey.

Listen to your inner voice.

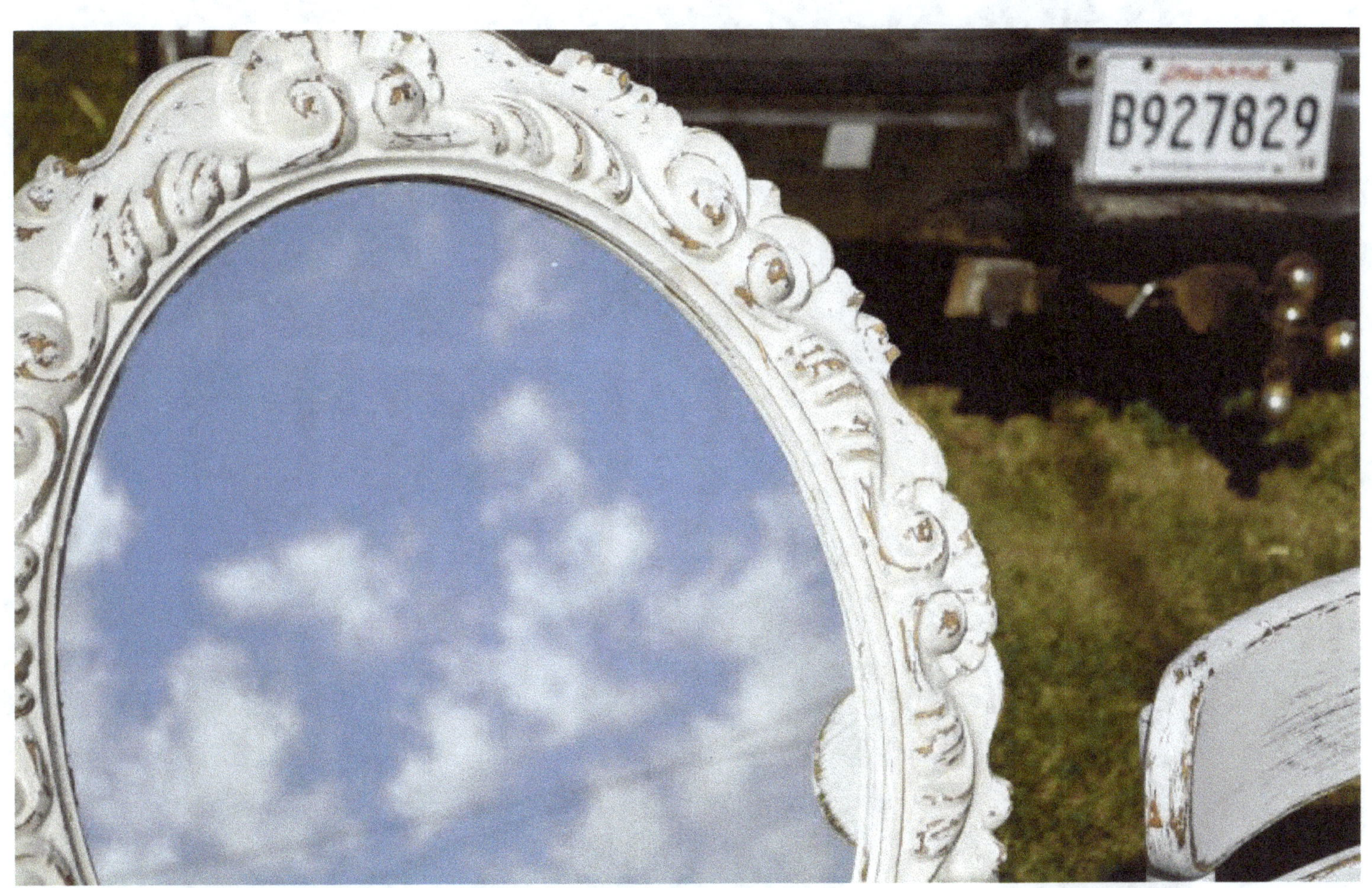

B927829

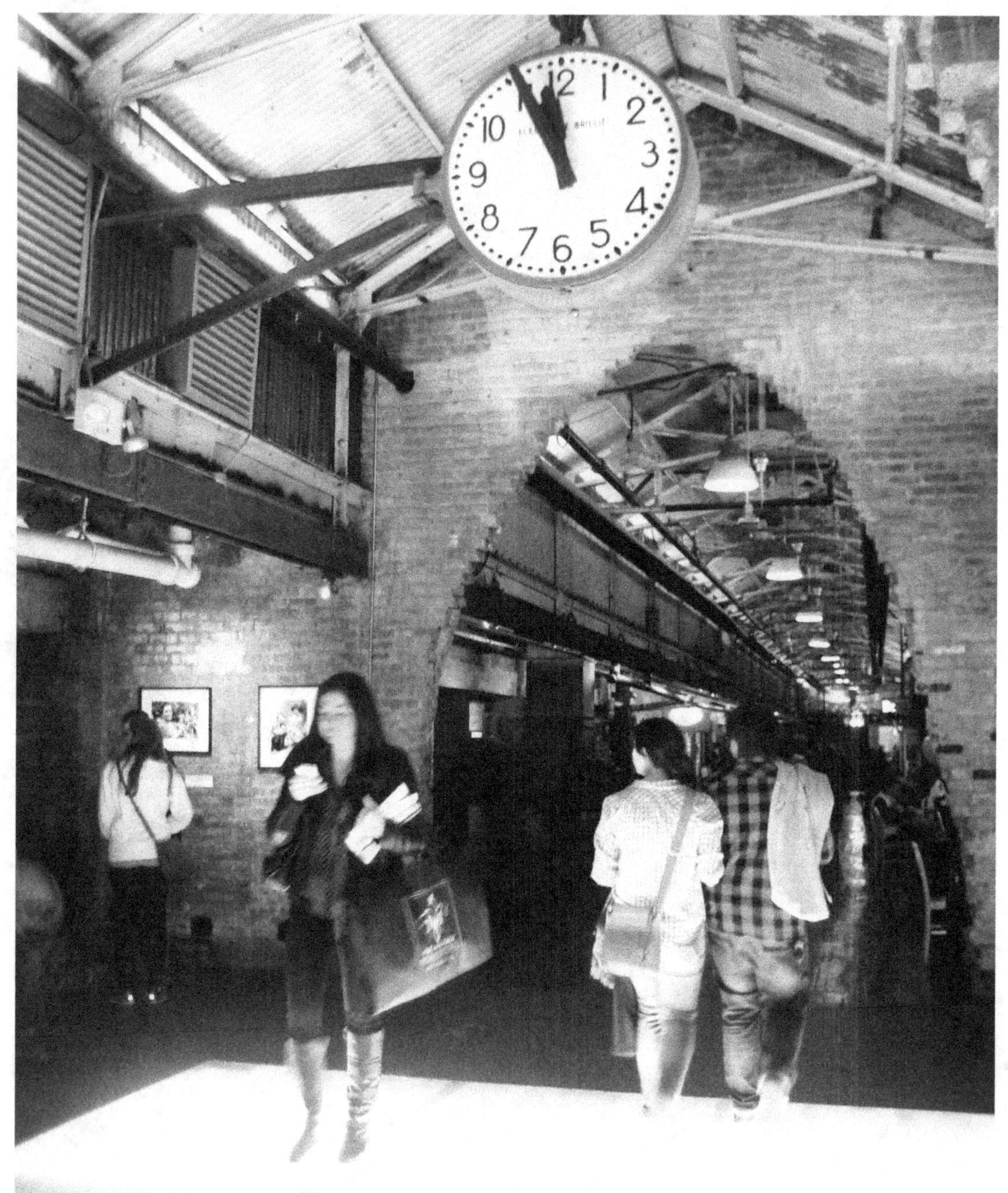

Stop for a moment.

Breathe.

This is your journey.

Deep inside resides a reservoir of strength.

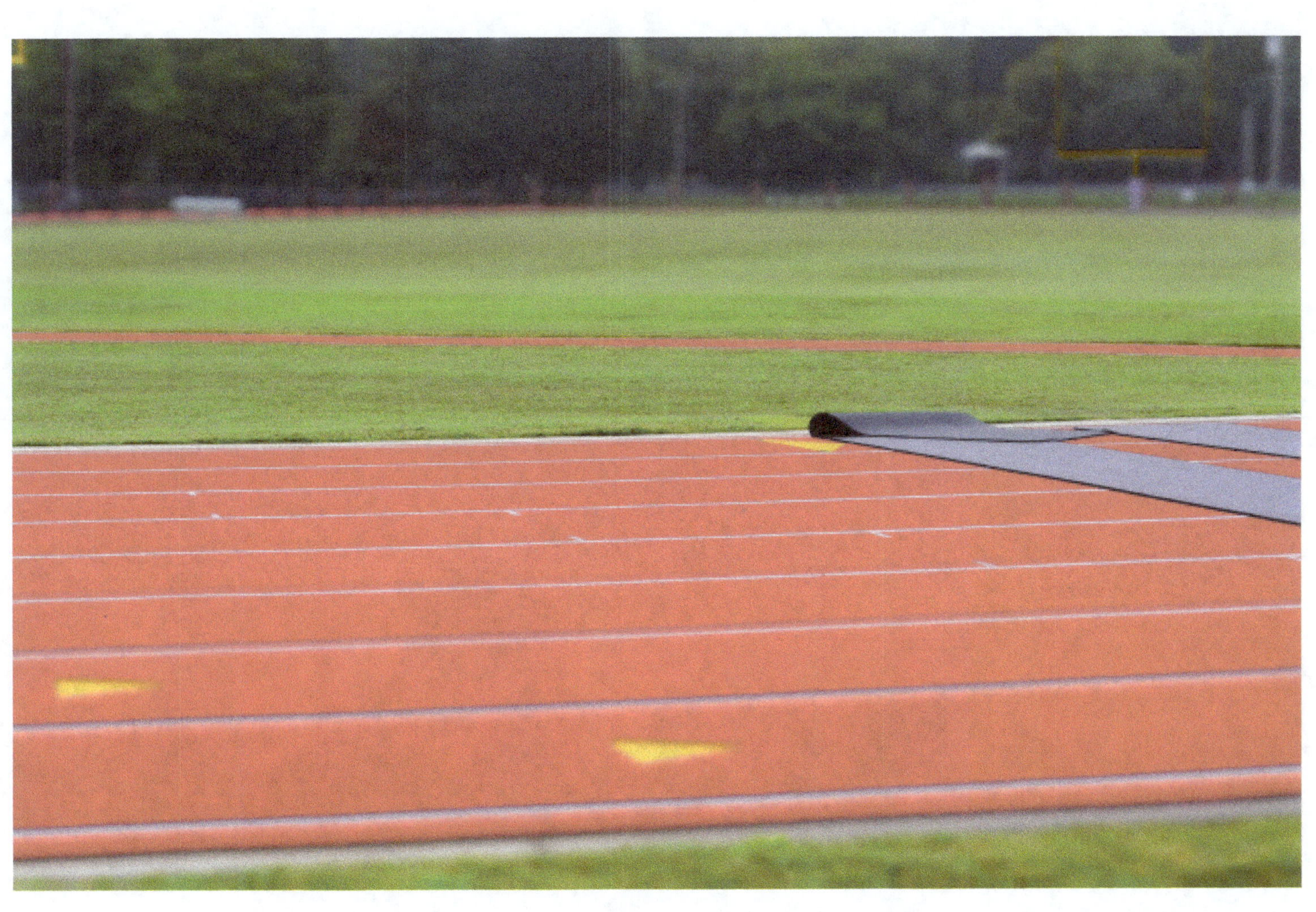

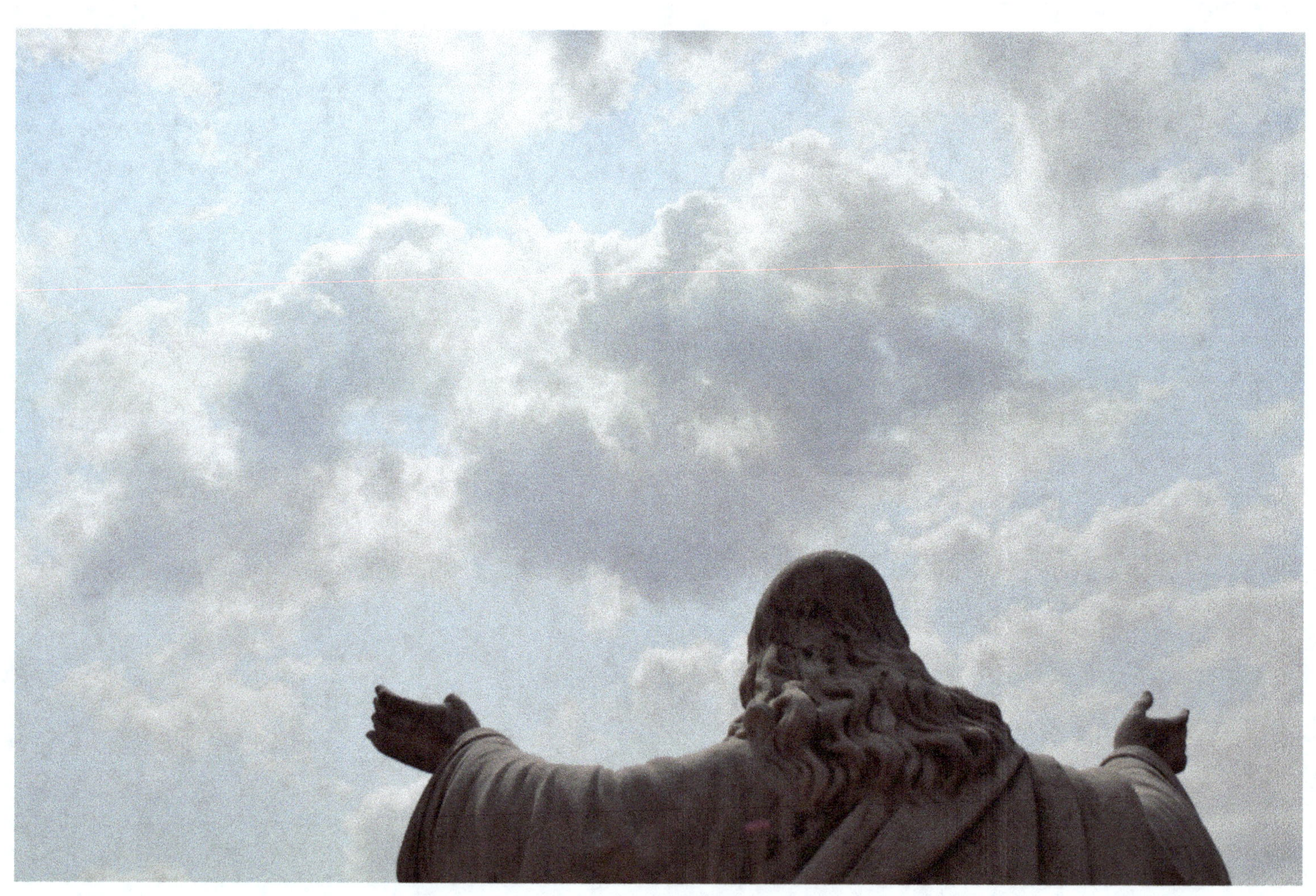

If I could come through the pages of this book and comfort you,
I would.

Give yourself and your partner space, respect, and love.

Healing will come from within.

This is your journey.

Feel surrounded by light.

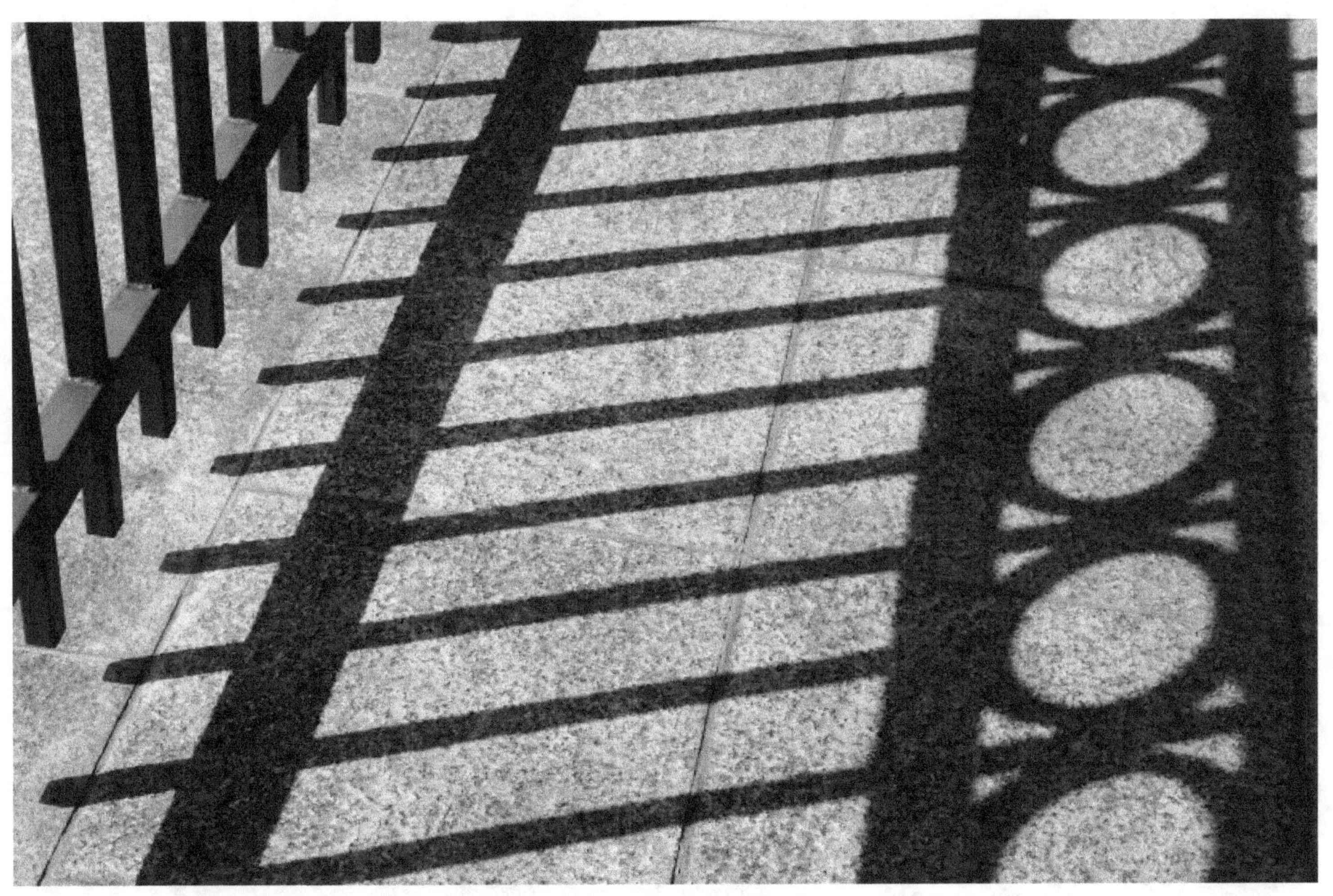

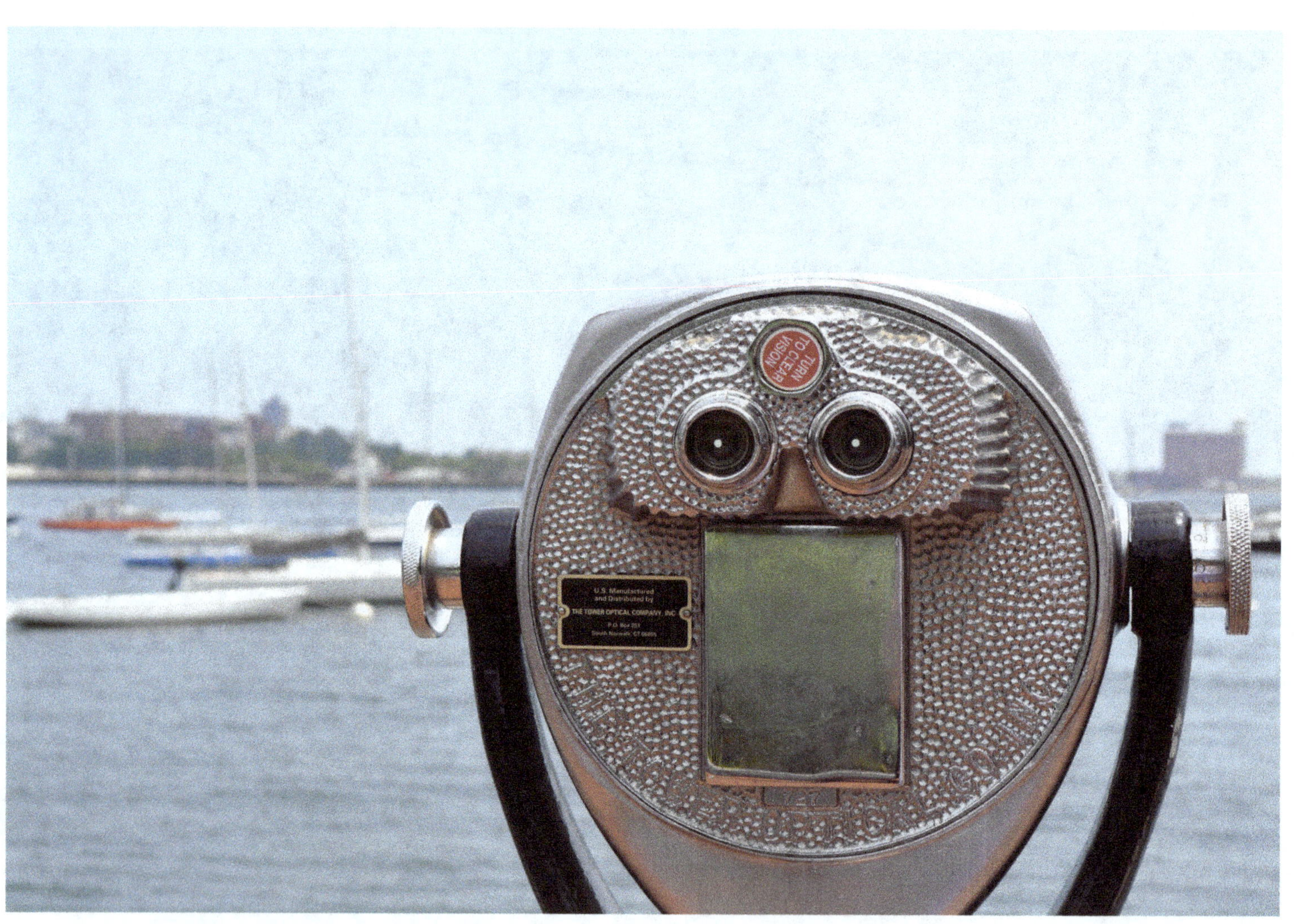

TURN TO CLEAR VISION
U.S. Manufactured
and Distributed by
THE TOWER OPTICAL COMPANY, INC
P.O. Box 251
South Norwalk, CT 06855

You may seek answers.

You may ask, "What did I do wrong?"

This is not your fault. It was nothing you did.

This is your journey.

Shower yourself with empathy.

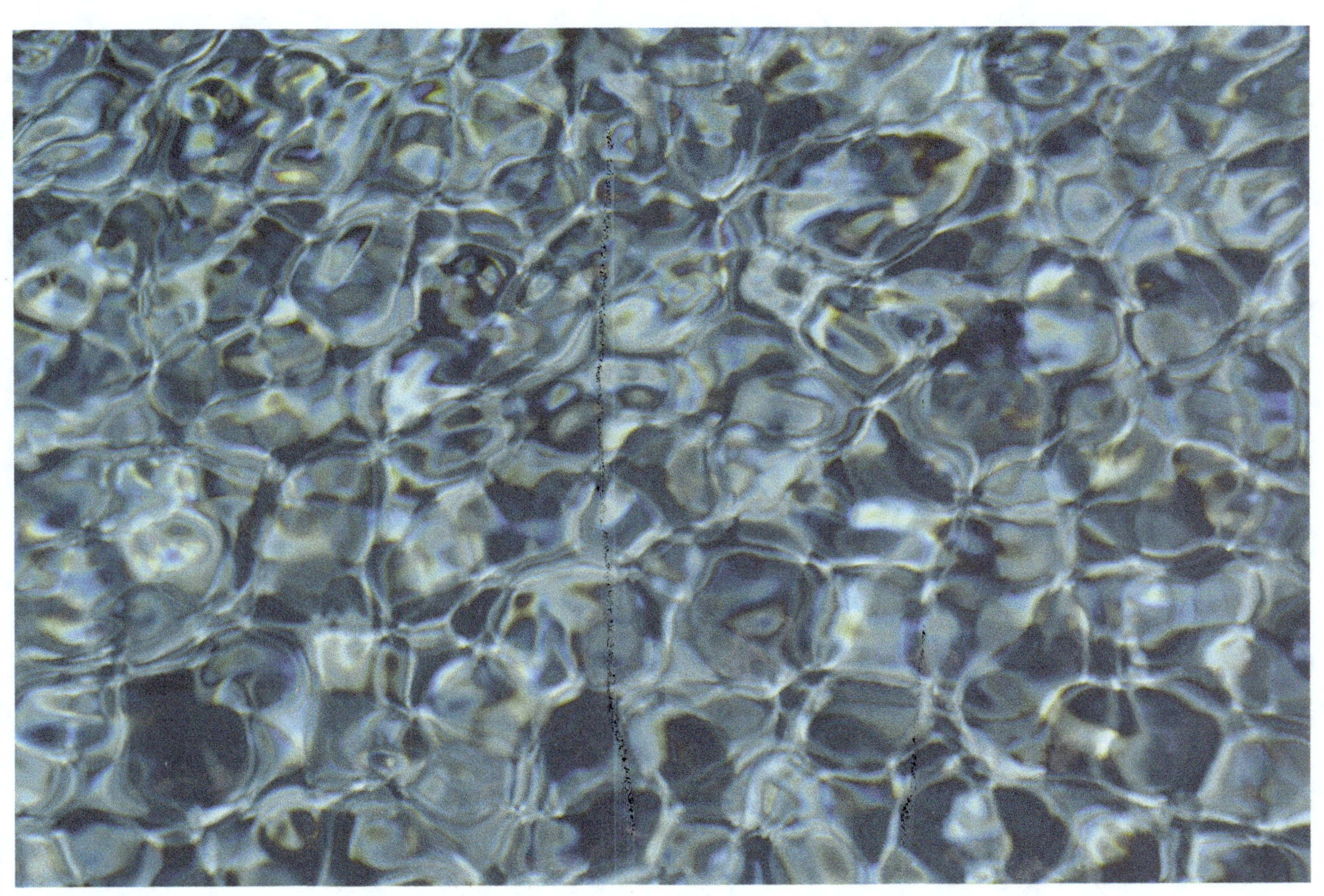

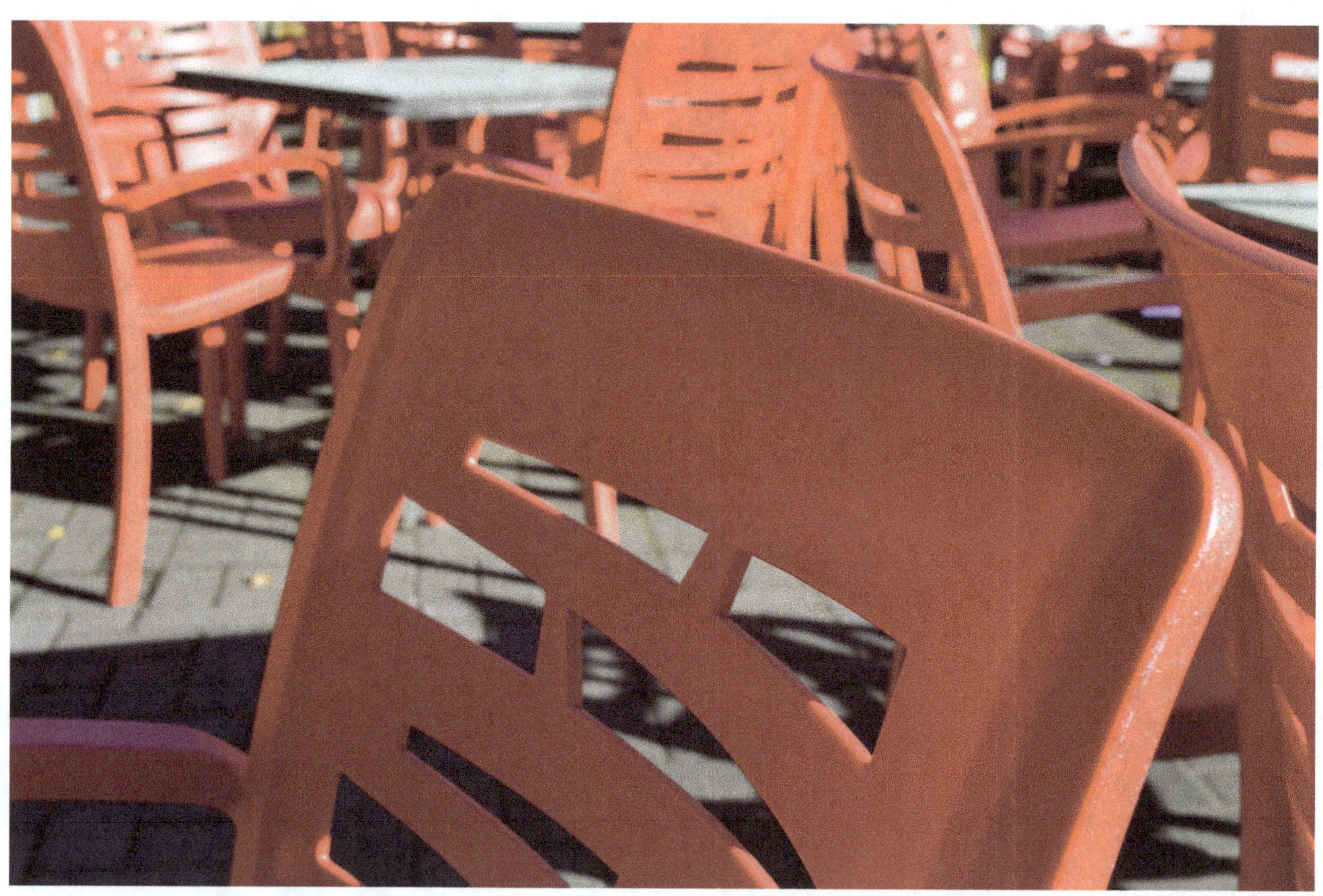

You are not alone.

Someone close to you may have gone through this trial as well.
Perhaps you didn't know until now.

She may want to help.
Ask her to simply be present and listen without judgment.

This is your journey.

A change of scenery may provide a sense of calm.

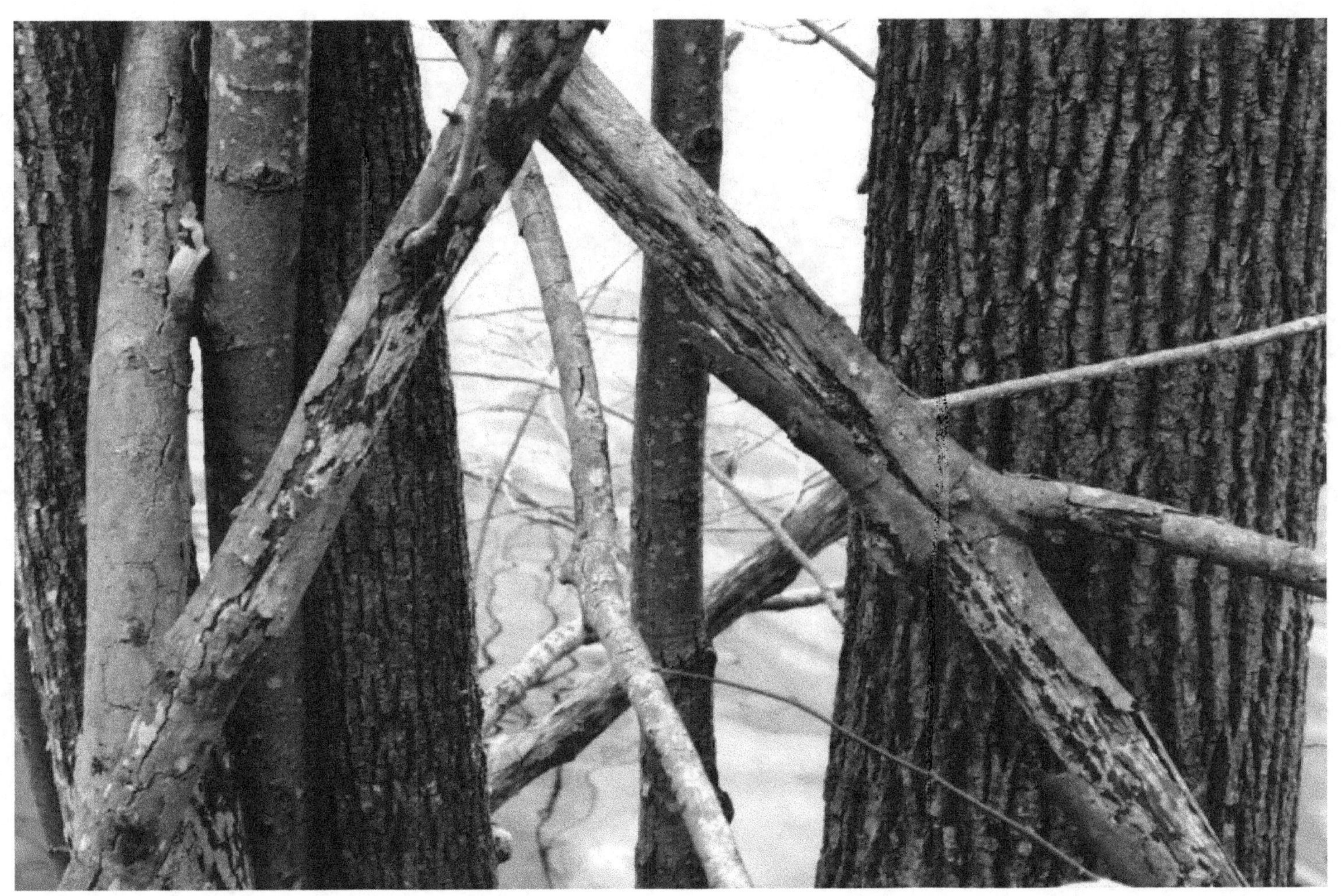

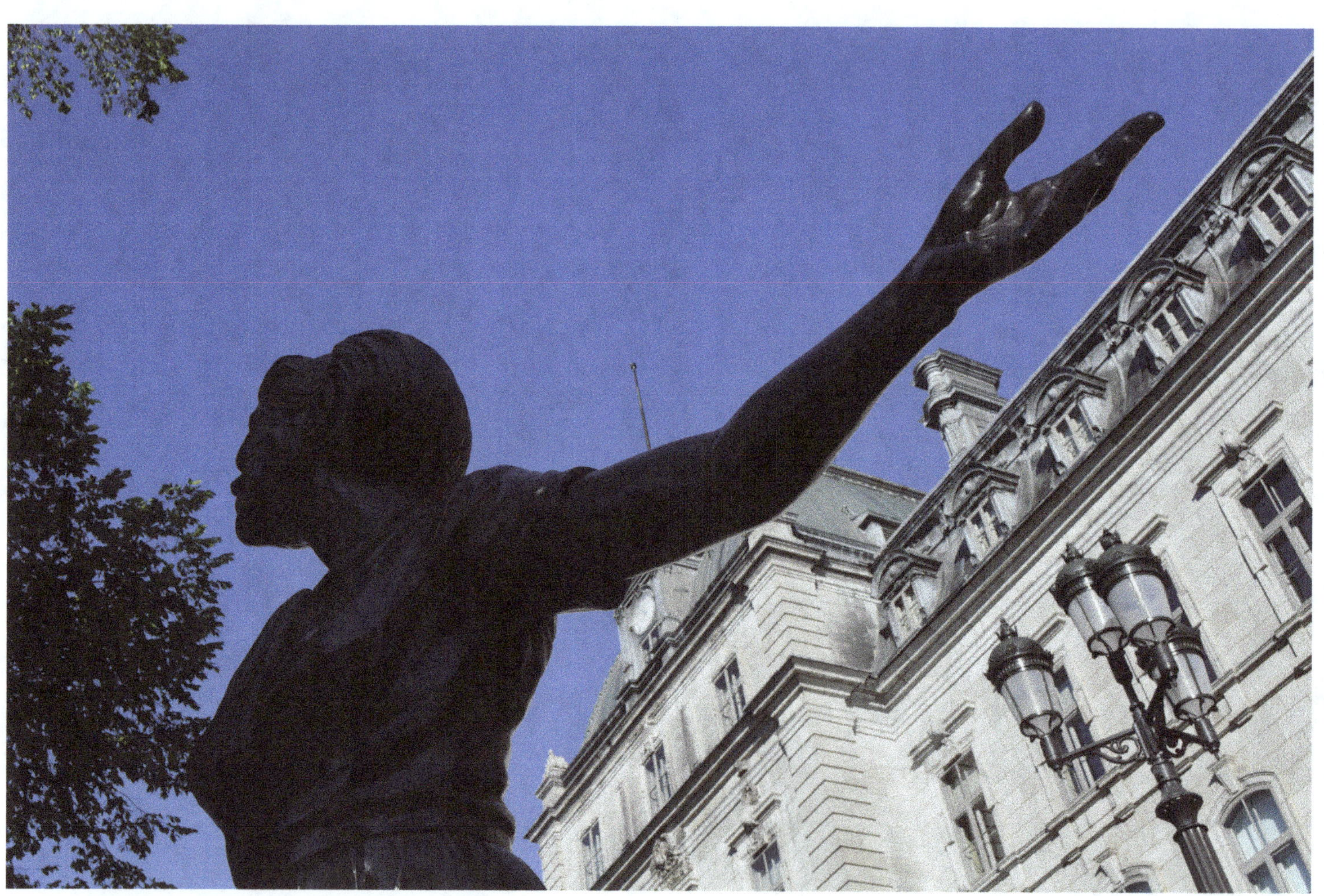

You might not feel it at this moment, but you will find your way through
and come out stronger.

This life mattered. Your story matters.

This is your journey. No one has lived your experience.

I am truly sorry for your loss.

My wish for you in moving forward is only peace.

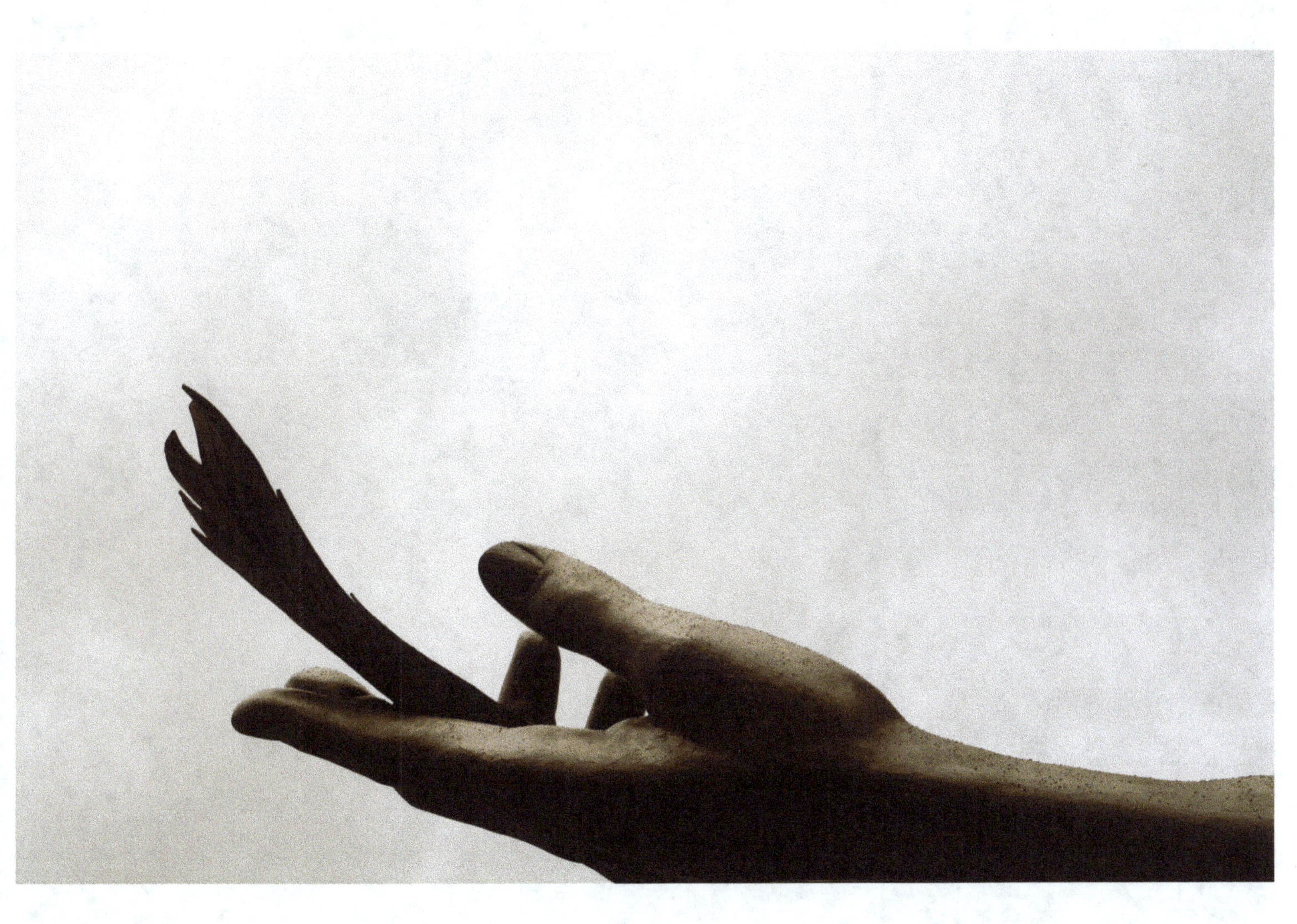

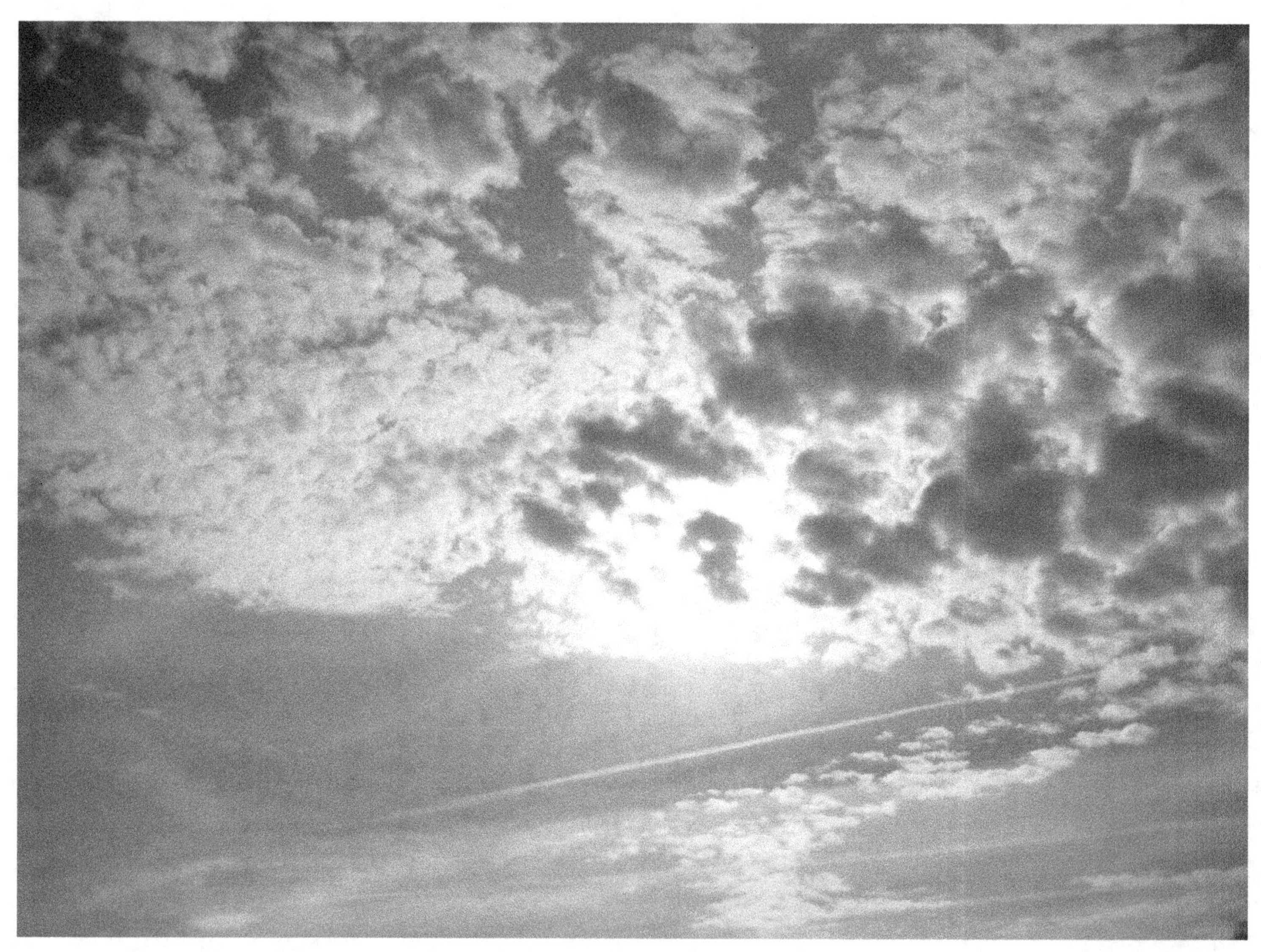

RESOURCES

Resolve
www.resolve.org

Hope After Loss
www.hopeafterloss.org

Share, Pregnancy & Infant Loss
Nationalshare.org

March of Dimes
www.marchofdimes.org

Lori E. Collins

While I am proud of my Midwestern roots, I'm equally proud to call myself a Nashvillian. I have a love for working out, taking photos, spending time with my hubby, teaching, volunteering, and eating good food. After experiencing pregnancy loss, I found that while people often had the best of intentions, they were unsure what to say or how best to support me. In writing this book, I thought about what I would want others to hear. We may not feel exactly the same, but my hope is that you will find some solace in this message. Everyone deserves the opportunity to express grief in whatever way comforts their soul.